THE REIGN OF LOVE

Other Andrew Murray titles:

The Reign of Love

(Selected Expositions from the Epistles)

ANDREW MURRAY

Edited by
Simon Fox

Collins

Marshall Pickering

First published in Great Britain in 1990 by Marshall Pickering

Marshall Pickering is an imprint of the Collins Religious Division, part of the Collins Publishing Group, 8 Grafton Street, London W1X 3LA

ISBN 0 7208 0748 4

Text set in Times by Watermark, Hampermill Cottage, Watford WD1 4PL
Printed in Great Britain by Cox & Wyman Ltd, Reading, Berks.

CONTENTS

1

Living Wholly for Christ

*For the love of Christ constraineth us;
because we thus judge, that if one died for
all, then all were dead: and that he died
for all, that they which live should not
henceforth live unto themselves, but unto
him which died for them, and rose again.*
2 Corinthians 5:14–15

There are two kinds of Christian. One kind lives
partly for himself and partly for Christ. The other
kind lives wholly for Christ. Jesus has stolen his
heart away to heaven. Oh, let us all say, 'Farewell,
accursed self; welcome, Christ, to my heart.' Paul
wrote, 'they which live should not henceforth live
unto themselves.' This means that we must deny

self and not retain a bit of self-will, self-seeking or self-honouring. How can we do this? To know that, we need to think about the words, 'unto him' in the verses quoted above. They mean that the death of Jesus has made it possible for us to live for him.

Many mothers make idols of their children and seem to live for them. They will do anything and everything for their welfare. Similarly, when the love of Jesus enters our hearts we only want to please him; we cannot bear the thought of grieving him. Then there follows the desire to know him and have fellowship with him. Just as the mother longs to be with her child, we long to live in the presence of Christ. And then there follows the life of dependence, in which we let Christ work in us.

In the old days at the Cape, when people kept slaves, even some of the ministers had them. Many of these slaves were very faithful people and would sacrifice their sleep and their health — yes, even their lives — for their masters. They were proud to be the slaves of ministers and loved to serve them. And in the same way, should we not long to do the will of our blessed Lord?

How can we attain to this sort of devotion to Christ? We can learn from the example of Paul. The Lord Jesus revealed himself to him from heaven, and this was the foundation of his Christian life. He saw the face which was brighter than the sun, and afterwards that face was in his mind's eye through all the trials of his life. You may say, 'If I could have a vision like Paul's I would be able to live wholly for Christ.' But God can enable you to live for him, even if you do not have a vision as dramatic as Paul's. Jesus took Paul as a sample or a pattern of what God could do to a man, saying to us through him, 'You can all copy that pattern.'

Having received the vision, Paul surrendered readily. 'Lord, what wilt thou have me to do?' he asked. We should not consecrate ourselves to happiness, or to an imaginary Jesus, but to the will of God. We need to say, 'Lord, I want to see your face and find out what your will is every day.' Do you think that is asking too much? It is the man who asks for more than he can get who gets most.

Where will this kind of life lead us? It can only lead us to Christ. Many Christians do not see a full Christ. Jesus means the salvation of the world. He means a heart which longs to save the world, which gives itself up to death for the sake of others. It is almost a forgotten truth that every person in the Church is meant to live for the salvation of men. I find I have to argue this point with others. It ought to need no arguing. Jesus went to Calvary in a spirit of self-sacrificing love. Do you imagine that when that same spirit enters your life it will be as a self-pleasing spirit? An old writer once said that if you take Christ into your heart you have to take the world into your heart as well. Christ, through the Spirit, offered himself to God; will that same Spirit lead you to do something different?

There is a great distance between the thing which takes the first place in your life and the thing which takes the second place. Jesus wants to be in the first place. Many feel satisfied with giving a little of their time or money, but Christ is not satisfied with that. He wants your whole being entirely for himself. Some of us are called to do missionary work overseas, and yet even those who are not so called and cannot go abroad because of family ties or other reasons, can still be willing to take the world into their hearts and to pray for the missionary work. We all need to say, 'Jesus, I long to live no longer for myself but wholly for you.'

2

Self-Denial

Even Christ pleased not himself.
Romans 15:3

There are many duties in the Christian life, such as prayer, reading God's Word, obedience, humility, love and self-denial. It is good to encourage these, but it is still better to lead people to the abundant life in Christ in which these duties are no longer a matter of argument and compulsion, but are the natural fruit of a heart which now delights in them.

This is especially true of self-denial. The very word suggests to many people the idea of doing something which they dislike or denying themselves a pleasure. But self-denial does not have to be like that. Indeed, for a healthy soul the greatest pleasure and delight of all is to deny itself. Don't we often consider it a privilege to deny ourselves for the sake of a friend on earth? Then surely the same would be the case with all that can be called self-denial if it were done for the sake of the love and friendship of our Holy Lord Jesus. To see how this can be we need to go to the very root of the matter and to understand the essence of true self-denial.

Revolution and revelation

We can all understand what a mental revolution is needed before a simple farmer, who still believes that the sun moves around the earth and that the earth stands still, can accept the idea that the reverse is in fact the case. It contradicts all that sense and reason teach him; the language of daily life all around him and that of the Bible itself are on his side. It has been justly said that a revolution something like this, only much greater, occurs when a sinner, to whom the visible world has been all-important and God insignificant, is caused by his conversion to see the world as insubstantial and unsatisfying and to give God and his salvation the first place in his thinking. When the Holy Spirit makes this change in a man's life, he may well cry out, 'I was guilty of the same stupidity as that of the ignorant countryman in making the earth the centre of my system, and giving God the second place. What blindness! I thought Time was more important than Eternity. Now I put Eternity first. Christ is my Sun and Centre.'

And yet in the lives of most Christians there is a need for another revolution, no less entire and no less difficult. It is true that a great change has already taken place, but it is only a beginning. They have indeed admitted the truth that God must come first and the world second. But as yet they are very far from understanding what that truth implies. There is one part of the worldly life which they have not yet recognised. It is the part of the kingdom of this world which each man carries within him – that is, his own *self*. In real terms the Christianity of very many believers, who have fled from the world and the destruction coming upon it, still consists in placing self first and God second. All they seek is their salvation and happiness. They have never got beyond saying, 'Some of self and some of Christ'. They have never dreamed that it is necessary, possible, desirable and truly blessed to say and to live the words, 'None of self and all of Christ'. A second revolution is needed to bring the believer to the stage where he lives entirely for Christ.

And how is this to come about? The revolution must be preceded by a revelation. As the ignorant farmer listened and by degrees was convinced by one proof after another, a new world opened up to him, and his whole outlook was changed. Something similar happens when someone is converted. The Holy Spirit opens the eyes of a man so that he sees his sin and danger in loving the world more than God, and this realisation brings about a change in attitude and life. Again, there must be a revelation before this revolution in the Christian life which we have been thinking about can take place. There must be a divine discovery by the believer of the place which is rightfully God's and of his claim to have *all* of the believer's heart and love and life, every moment and in every thing. There must be a realisation of the terrible sinfulness of the self, which has kept God out of his place and has in reality ruled so much of the believer's life, when he was under the illusion all the while that he was truly earnest in serving God.

No argument could convince the farmer as long as his self-confidence made him unwilling to be taught. No preaching can change the sinner until a desire to know God's truth is awakened in him. And the same desire is also needed in believers.

Deliverance from self

Are you willing, my reader, to listen to God's message about self? Or do you believe that you are in no way pleasing, trusting or honouring self? Are you sure that in your very acts of so-called self-denial you are not secretly giving place to God's enemy? May each of us pray that God will make us willing to discover the self in us which needs to be denied.

What is self? It is man's God-given power of knowing and controlling himself. What is the task which self is meant to do? God gave man this self so that he might have the power and the honour of voluntarily acknowledging his blessed dependence upon God and receiving everything which God, in his love, is delighted to give him. For this reason Christ constantly gave up his self to God. He did nothing in his own power: 'even Christ pleased not himself' (Rom. 15:3).

And when does the self become sinful? When self, which God gave us so that we might turn to him, turns from him to itself, seeking its own life and pleasure and honour. This self is indeed the power of sin and Satan; it is the source and strength of all sin; it is the subtle power by which everything – even our worship and work for God, even our self-denial and humility – can be made the food of pride and self-righteousness.

And how are we to be delivered from this self? Christ said, 'Let a man deny himself, and take up his cross' (Matt. 16:24). The cross means the curse and death. Jesus was saying that a man must deny his right to have anything to say about his life; he must give his self to death on the cross. Self deserves death: there is no deliverance from it except through death. In the death of Christ our old man or self was crucified. Not that self dies, but we die to it. In Christ's death to sin, we died, and now we can say, 'I, in my old self, live no more, but Christ lives in me instead; and I, in my new self, live by the faith of the Son of God. I have given the old self on the cross to the curse; in Christ I am freed from it.' The new self lives in Christ; it lives in a new heart, in which Christ, the Spirit and the love of God dwell. It delights in giving all it has to the One who died and now lives for us. It loves to ask the question, 'Lord Jesus, what else can I do for you? What new sacrifice can I bring to you?'

There has been a revelation of the cursed nature of the monstrous old self which usurped the place of God, a revelation of the evil and ruin which it causes in my life, of its subtle and unceasing deceit in leading me to do my own will instead of God's. I now see that the old self has been the cause of all my failure and unhappiness, and with my whole heart I judge it deserving of death on the cross. There has been a revelation of the wonderful power of the new, Christlike self to yield itself wholly and continually to God, and of the inexpressible privilege and blessing of doing so. I now see the evil of gratifying the old self and the joy of denying it. This revelation causes a revolution in my faith and life: the evil self, with its every desire, is nailed to the cross; God on the Throne, with Christ, is my All in All; the new self only lives in order to bring all it can find and lay it at his feet. The new self delights in self-denial.

This is the root from which true self-denial grows. It has many branches and fruits, such as refusing to gratify the pleasures of the flesh, giving ourselves to a continual ministry of love to help others, making pleasing God our chief desire and putting our time, thought, position and abilities at God's disposal. As we practise self-denial we discover that it is a joy to give up everything for God.

Self-denial and money

I particularly want us to think about the giving of our money as a part of self-denial. The first thing we need to consider is Christ's teaching on this subject in the Sermon on the Mount, in which he told us to give in secret, with no desire to please ourselves or others. We should give knowing that the Father sees our giving, and that in giving we gain his guidance and approval. We should give knowing that he will reward us, that he will bless both us and the gift which we give. A careful study of this teaching and a full acceptance of it will help us with our self-denial.

We should remember that giving is most definitely a divine command. The spirit and the measure of God's own giving is put before us as the measure for ours: 'Freely ye have received, freely give' (Matt. 10:8). 'It is more blessed to give than to receive' (Acts 20:35). 'As I have done unto you, do ye also.' Our giving should be like God's giving. By giving in this way we express the divine love, and we bring blessing to men and thanksgiving to God.

Perhaps you think the joy of self-denial which I have been talking about is beyond your reach. But won't you at least aim at it? Won't you ask yourself whether in what you spend on yourself and your family you are pleasing the old self more than Jesus? You may say that it is difficult to answer that question. I do not doubt it. But that is only all the more reason for asking it and taking time to answer it. You were created and redeemed with the one purpose of being a pleasure to God in everything you do. He wants to be able to say to each of his children, 'You are my beloved son, in whom I am well pleased.' Do not turn away with the thought that it will be too much trouble to find out whether you are giving just what pleases the Father or whether you are instead pleasing and nourishing the evil self.

Are you content to leave undecided the question of whether God or self really has the guiding voice in the spending of your money? If you are, isn't that a proof that you have reason to fear that self has too much of its own way? Oh, do not let the sun and the earth, God and the self, take each other's rightful place. Do not be afraid to say, 'To please God is my greatest pleasure, and self-denial is itself a pleasure if through it I can please God.'

You may frequently hear calls for financial help for missionary work. God's servants in the mission fields are giving their whole lives with joy for the name of Jesus, and they sorely need your help. Are you taking part in the infinite self-sacrifice of Jesus and in the loving self-denial of his servants, always giving as much as you can to his work, ready to give anything if you think it will please him? This has been said so many times that one is almost reluctant to say it again: there are millions of heathens perishing in the world. Won't you for their sake deny yourself a little more than you have done? You cannot please Jesus more than by loving and caring for the souls of the perishing. Ask youself, 'What am I doing to please the Lord in this, and what more can I do?'

The real fruit of self-denial only grows on the root of death to self and a life which is wholly devoted to God. There is no joy more exquisite than that of self-denial, than that of denying yourself something which would have pleased you, for the far higher pleasure of pleasing Jesus.

3

Indwelt by God

> *And what agreement hath the temple of God with idols? For ye are the temple of the living God; as God hath said, I will dwell in them, and walk in them; and I will be their God, and they shall be my people.*
>
> 2 Corinthians 6:16

Here we have an answer to the question, 'How is God going to be my God?' Many Christians ask it, and often they wonder, 'Should I regard him as a great, almighty, distant God in heaven, outside me and separate from me, who will from time to time give me help?' That is what many Christians think, and because they see God this way they experience little of his real presence and power. No, this picture of God is only the beginning of true faith in him. As we get to know Scripture better and we begin to appreciate the deep needs of our hearts and understand the wonderful love of God which longs to enter completely into us, we learn that there is something better. The question, 'How is God going to be my God?' finds its answer in these words: 'God hath said, I will dwell in them, and I will be their God.'

And what a wonderful answer it is. There are things in life which surround us and yet never get inside our hearts, and there are other things which enter into us and take possession of our very lives. A mother has a place for her child in her heart — it lives there. The gold of a miser has a special place in his heart. Our hearts were actually created so that God might live in them, that he might give his life and love there, and that there our love and joy might be in him alone. How little we appreciate the fact that just as we have the love of husbands, wives, parents and children filling our hearts and making us happy, so too we can have the love of the Living God, for whom the heart was made, dwelling in it and filling it with his own goodness and blessing. This is the message I want to get across: God wants your heart. If you give it to him, he will live in it.

To the Psalmist, God was his God, his strength and his 'exceeding joy' (Ps. 43:4). But how is God to be my God, my strength and my joy? In no other way than by coming into my life with his divine life, and filling me with his almighty strength. With his holy life and love he comes into my heart, the very seat and centre of my being, and works within me as my God, ordering my life for me. He divinely and blessedly fulfils the promise to dwell in me and be my God.

Don't you think it would make a wonderful difference to our lives if we really believed this promise, and by believing received the blessing which it speaks of? What a holy awe there would be in us, and what a tender fear we would have of hurting or grieving this holy, loving God. What a longing would be awakened in us. Our hearts would say, 'I want to know how to walk with this God and have full communion with him.' And what a bright confidence we would have: 'Now that my God has come to dwell in me, I need no longer fear that I shall not have his presence, or that he will not do for me and in me everything that I need.'

I want to explain this indwelling by God very simply, and to show that it is the very essence of true Christianity — the very thing which man as a sinner needed to have restored to him, and the very thing which Christ Jesus came to give.

Creation and the indwelling by God

It was for nothing less and nothing else than this indwelling that man was created by God. Have you ever wondered why God created man at all? God brought him into existence so that he might reveal and impart his own divine goodness and glory to man, so that man, as far as he were capable of it, might share God's divine perfections and blessedness. And God especially created man in his own image and likeness so that in man he might show

how he could dwell in the human creature, and gradually fit him and lift him up for dwelling with God and in God throughout eternity. God's love said, 'In his measure, I want man to be as holy and as good and as blessed as I am. I cannot give him the holiness or blessedness apart from myself, but I can and will dwell in him, in the inmost depths of his life, and be to him his goodness and his strength.' Yes, this was the glory of the divine creating love: God wanted to give man all that he had himself; God gave himself to be man's life and joy.

God could not do this except by dwelling in him. A lamp has a light inside it which through the glass gives out light. In a similar way the God of love was to be the inner light of man's life. It was to be man's dignity and blessedness that in and through him all the glories of the Blessed God should for ever shine out in the universe. Our whole nature — will, feelings, abilities — was to be the vessel which was to receive and hold and overflow with the wonderful fullness of the life of God. And it was to be man's high prerogative and privilege to offer and yield himself to God in the consciousness of this holy partnership. What God was in himself in heaven, that he was to be on earth in and through man, living out his life in him as truly as he lived it out in heaven. Oh, the wonder of being human! Let us give glory to the God of our creation.

But now let us consider the promise, 'I will dwell in them,' in the light of what sin has done. God had made man to be his home, his temple, where his presence and his will would be all in all. But sin robbed both man and God of this indwelling. The temptation with which Satan came to man in

Paradise really meant this: would he with his whole heart yield to God as Father and Master, giving him his rightful place and doing only his will? Or would he do his own will, and let self rule as master? Tragically, man made the wrong choice. God was dethroned and cast out of his temple. Self was enthroned on the seat of God, just as in later days the image of an idol was set up in the very home which God had caused to be built for himself in Jerusalem.

The biblical description of the man of sin, when he is fully revealed and arrived at full maturity — 'who opposeth and exalteth himself above all that is called God, or that is worshipped; so that he as God sitteth in the temple of God, shewing himself that he is God' (2 Thess. 2:4) — is also a description of the sinful self in every age and place. Self sits in the temple of God as God. All the sin of heathendom (and how awful it is!) and all the sin of Christendom (no less terrible!) is just the outgrowth of that one root: God dethroned and self enthroned in the heart of man. All the sin and sorrow of each one of us is in essence this: we were not what we were created to be; we did not have God dwelling in our hearts to fill them with his life, peace and love.

Would anyone be happy to permit loathsome reptiles to live in his house? Would he allow someone else to be the master in his home? Of course not. And yet Christians allow so many things other than God to occupy their hearts and have the place which is meant for God alone. And most are quite unaware that they are doing this. I want to convey this message: let there be an end to all this desecration of God's temple. God asks to have your whole heart for himself. Oh, let him have it!

Redemption and the indwelling by God

Let us for a moment consider this indwelling by God in the light of Christ's work of redemption. What was the purpose of Christ's coming from heaven? It was to show us the possibility and the blessedness of being a man indwelt by God. When God's Son became a man, he lived a perfect human life, even though he was 'made like us in all things'. He told us that he did it by the power of the Father, who dwelt in him: 'I do nothing of myself — the Father in me doeth the work.' This is not a matter of abstract thought or deep theology. Here was a real man — hungry, weary, tempted, weeping, suffering like ourselves — telling us that the Father lived in him, and that this was the secret of his perfect, blessed life. He felt it all just as we feel it, but he could do and bear anything because the Father was in him. He showed us how a man can live perfectly, and how God can enable us to do it.

Once he had done this in his life, he died so that he might deliver us from the power of sin and open up the way for us to return to God. On the cross he proved that a man in whom God dwells will be ready to suffer anything and to give up his life even to the point of death, so that he may enter into the fullness of the life of God. When sin had entered him man had lost the indwelling life of God and had become dead to it. There was no way for man to be freed from the life of sin except by dying to it. Christ died to sin, so that he might take us up into his fellowship and that we too might be dead to sin. Then we could live for God with Christ's life. So he won back for us the God-indwelt life for which man had been created by giving us his own life, the very life he had lived.

My beloved fellow Christians, this is the salvation which Christ has won for us: a deliverance from self by death to it through the death on the cross; a restoration to the life which we were created for, with our hearts made into a home for God.

Pentecost and the indwelling by God

And how are we to become partakers of this salvation? To answer that question we need to consider this wonderful truth of the divine indwelling in the light of Pentecost and the coming of the Holy Spirit. Have you understood the meaning of God's sending the Holy Spirit into our hearts? It is nothing less than this: Christ, who had been with the disciples on earth but not in them, now came back to them in the Spirit to dwell in them, just as he had before dwelt with them. We read of a wonderful change coming over the disciples. Their selfishness was changed into love, their pride into humility, their fear of suffering into boldness and joy, their unbelief into fullness of faith, their feebleness into power. And it was all due to this one thing: the glorified Christ had come to dwell within them as their life. There was joy in heaven at Pentecost. God had regained possession of his temple and could now dwell in men as he had meant to do before the Fall. As Christ had foretold, the temple of his earthly body was broken down when he died upon the cross for our sins. The temple which he was to build in three days was his resurrection body, with its holy, heavenly life. In union with it, we are now the temple of the Living God. The Holy Spirit takes possession of us, God's temple, in the name of the Three-in-One God, and the Father and the Son come to make their home with us.

When we look at the great promise, 'I will dwell in them,' and its fulfilment at Pentecost, we are reminded of the great difference between the preparatory working of the Spirit in conversion and regeneration, and his Pentecostal indwelling. Every Christian must have the former: without it there is no life. But it is only the preparation of the temple. Pentecost is the glory of God filling the temple, God coming to dwell in the heart. Let us believe that the promise can and will be fulfilled.

In the light of God's promise to dwell in us, let us look at the state of the Church of Christ. There are many believers of whom one could never say that their hearts are temples which God has cleansed and where he dwells. There is so much coldness, worldliness, selfishness, sin and inconsistency that one sometimes wonders if there are any real Christians at all. The state of the Church is indeed sad. How little zeal there is for God's honour, how little delight in his fellowship, how little devotion to his service and kingdom, how little life in the power of the Holy Spirit. This all surely proves that God's promise to dwell in us has never been understood, believed or claimed by a large majority of Christians.

Have you claimed this promise? This is the way to do it: begin by confessing how little you have even tried to live as God's temple. Think of how it must have grieved the heart of your Father that after all he has done through his Son and his Spirit to get his dwelling place back again, you have cared very little about it. Also confess your helplessness. You have tried to be better than you are, and you have failed. You will fail until you believe that nothing less is needed than that God himself should become the strength of your life. Also believe that nothing less than this is offered by God.

Set your heart upon this blessing from God. Desire is the great moving power of the world; fix your desire upon the wonderful promise that God will dwell in you. Let no thought of your unworthiness or feebleness discourage you. This is something which is impossible with man, but with God it is possible. He can and will fulfil his promise. Let it become the one desire of your heart. Understand that this is the salvation which the Holy Spirit brings you as soon as you are ready to give up everything for it. As soon as the heart is ready to lose all, to be cleansed from all that is of self or nature, the promise will surely be fulfilled.

We should carefully heed the words which follow God's promise: 'Wherefore come out from among them, and be ye separate, saith the Lord, and touch not the unclean thing; and I will receive you' (2 Cor. 6:17). Come out from everything that is of the world, even worldly religion. Come out from all that is inconsistent with the privilege of being God's holy temple and dwelling. Come out and be separate, take your stand as one who is going to live a life different from that of the crowd around you. Be separated to God and his will. 'And touch not the unclean thing' — be a cleansed temple where nothing which defiles even in the least may enter. Be wholly for God and holy to God, and he will make good his promise to dwell in you. He himself will reveal and impart and maintain within you all that the promise means.

Believer, will you accept this full salvation? Will you do it now? I pray that you will not reject this wonderful love. Oh, let your God have you, so that he may satisfy his love and yours by dwelling in you. Accept his love right now, and trust him to fulfil his promise.

4

Jesus Christ in You

Examine yourselves, whether ye be in the faith; prove your own selves. Know ye not your own selves, how that Jesus Christ is in you, except ye be reprobates?
2 Corinthians 13:5

Every thoughtful Bible reader knows that the state of the Corinthian church was a very sad one. There were terrible sins among them, and both of the epistles are full of Paul's sorrow and rebuke. At the close of the second epistle he sums up all his pleadings in the question quoted above. He is saying, 'Don't you know (I fear you don't, or else you would live differently) that unless you are entirely reprobate, *Jesus Christ is in you*?' These words teach us that what will lift a Christian out of sin and sloth is the great promise of God's indwelling, the awareness that Jesus Christ is in him.

'Know ye not your own selves?' Every Christian needs to know himself. He needs to know his own sinfulness and helplessness, but much more than that, he needs to understand the divine miracle which has taken place within him and made him the temple and dwelling of the Three-in-One God. We should learn above everything to know our own selves, to know that Jesus Christ is in us. In every Christian community there are some people who are living a low and feeble life, without joy or power over sin or the ability to bless others. To all such people Paul is here saying, 'Pause and listen, and take in the wonderful thought that will be for you the motive and the power to live an entirely new life: *Christ is in you.*' If you simply learn to believe this and to give way to it and to yield yourself to him, he will do his mighty saving work in you.

There are two great questions which we need to think about at this juncture. The first is, How is it that so many Christians fail? The answer is that they do not truly know that Jesus Christ is in them. Not one of us could live a worldly life — giving way to pride, selfishness and temper and grieving the Holy Spirit of God — if he really knew that Jesus Christ was in him. The effect of this knowledge would be simply wonderful. On the one hand it would sober and humble the believer and cause him to say, 'I cannot bear the thought of grieving the Christ within me.' On the other hand it would encourage and strengthen him to say, 'Praise God,

I have Jesus Christ within me! He will live my life for me!' May God bring us to confess how much we have lost because we have lacked this knowledge, and teach us to pray that from moment to moment our lives may express the truth that Jesus Christ is in us.

The other question we need to think about is this: If I find that I have not lived life in such a way, am I ready to say now, 'From now on, by the grace of God, I will; I can rest content with nothing less than the full experience of Jesus Christ dwelling in me'? We need to come to him in deep poverty and emptiness, trusting that the One who did the work so perfectly for us on Calvary promises to do it in our hearts too. May God, by the Holy Spirit, reveal to each of us all that he means us to enjoy.

Accept the indwelling Christ

If you want to live this life we are thinking of, you must *believe in and accept the indwelling Christ*. Do you fully and truly believe in such a Christ? You do believe in an incarnate Christ. When the name of Christ is mentioned, you at once think of the One who was born at Bethlehem, who took our nature upon him and lived as a man upon earth. That thought is inseparable from your faith in him. You also believe in the crucified Christ, who died on Calvary for our sins. You believe, too, in the risen Saviour, who lives for evermore. And you believe in the glorified Lord, who now sits on the throne of heaven. But do you believe as definitely and naturally in the indwelling Christ? Have you made his indwelling an article of your faith, as surely as you believe in Christ incarnate, crucified, risen and glorified? It is only as the truth of his indwelling is accepted that you can really profit from these other beliefs. Our experience of the love and saving power of our Lord depends entirely upon his indwelling us in order to reveal his presence and to do his work.

If your spiritual life is feeble and sickly, you may be sure that it is because you do not know that Jesus Christ is in you. You should at once begin to say, 'With my whole heart I want to take possession of and be possessed by the wonderful knowledge that Jesus Christ is in me — I want to know this not as a doctrine, but as an experience.' Begin to believe it at once. Accept Jesus right now as an indwelling Saviour. Day by day be content with nothing less than the blessed awareness of his indwelling presence. He loves to reveal himself.

A man always, to some extent, makes his home the expression of his tastes and character. In a similar way the Lord Jesus brings the heart which accepts and trusts him to dwell within it into sympathy and harmony with himself. How does he do this? The answer is not difficult. He becomes your life, he lives in you. Your thoughts, attitudes, emotions and actions — everything which is implied by that wonderful word 'life' — will all have his life and Spirit breathing in them. Oh, Christians who have never truly understood that Jesus Christ is in you, believe in him, accept him now as the indwelling Saviour.

Accept the whole Christ

When you accept Christ to dwell in you, be sure that you *accept the whole Christ*. There are some people who long for the indwelling Christ, but think of him chiefly as one who comes to comfort them and make them glad, to bring peace and joy to them. They do not accept him in his full character and majesty. Beware of being content with only half a Christ; see to it that you have the whole Christ. There are people who accept Christ as a Priest to atone for their sins, but they do not yield to his rule as a King; they never think of giving their own will to him, wholly and entirely. They come to Christ for happiness but not for holiness. They trust in the work which he has done for them, but they do not surrender themselves to him so that he may do the work which he wishes to do in them. They speak of the forgiveness of sins, but they know little of cleansing from all unrighteousness. They have not accepted the whole Christ, who is the Saviour from the power of sin as much as from the guilt of sin.

Let me urge you to make a study of this. As you read about the life of Christ on earth, look upon every trait of his holy character as what God wants for you. Study his holy humility and meekness and say, 'This is the Christ who dwells in me.' Think of his holy dependence upon the Father and the perfect surrender of his will to the Father's and say, 'I have yielded myself so that my indwelling Lord may bring about the same attitude in me too.' As you gaze upon him as the Crucified One, do not think of the cross only as an atonement, as the means of the propitiation of your sins, but think of it also as the means of victory over sin — think of the fellowship of the cross. Beware of only ever saying, 'Christ crucified for me'; say also, 'I am crucified with Christ.' The one reason why he lives in you is so that he may breathe his own likeness into your nature and give to you his own spirit of crucifixion, that blessed attitude of the heart which made his sacrifice so pleasing to the Father. Do receive the whole Christ to dwell in you.

Especially, do not forget that the Christ who is in you is the Loving One, the Servant and the Saviour of the lost. The chief mark and glory of the Son of God is that he lived and died not for himself but for others. When he comes to dwell in you, he does not change his nature; it is the crucified, redeeming love of God which takes possession of you. Yield yourself to him so that he may breathe into you his own love for souls, his own willingness to give up everything so that they may be saved, his own faith in God's almighty, conquering grace. Accept a whole Christ, a Saviour from all sin and selfishness — a Saviour not only for yourself but for all those around you.

Accept Christ with your whole heart

If you accept the whole, indwelling Christ, *accept him with your whole heart*. Nothing less than this can satisfy God, or secure Christ's full indwelling, or give our hearts rest. This was what even the Old Testament demanded: 'Thou shalt love the Lord thy God with all thine heart, and with all thy soul, and with all thy might' (Deut. 6:5). To this love alone was given the promise, 'Blessed are they

which seek him with their whole heart'. So how
can we even think that the wonderful New Testament blessing of the whole, indwelling Christ can
be experienced in power unless we give our whole
hearts to him?

What does it mean to accept the indwelling
Christ with one's whole heart? First of all, it means
that we must give Christ our love and affection.
Our relationship to him must not only be one of
trust in his help and devotion to his service, but also
one of intense personal attachment. The attitude of
his heart towards us is all love; his work was and is
nothing but the revelation of infinite love and ten-
derness. Nothing but love on our part can be the
proof that we have really accepted and known his
love. After Peter had denied Christ, his restoration
to Jesus' favour and to his place as the shepherd of
Christ's flock all hinged on his answer to the question which Jesus asked him three times: 'Lovest
thou me?' (John 21:15–17). We should not imagine
that it is only for women and children, mystics and
saints, to speak the language of tender, fervent love
to the Saviour. If we accept him with our whole
hearts, let us cultivate an intense personal love for
him. We should not hesitate to say often, 'Thou
knowest that I love thee.' Accepting Jesus with
one's whole heart means loving him with all one's
strength.

It also means giving up one's will to him entirely
and absolutely. Tell yourself that it is a settled matter that you will never seek your own will in anything. In things both great and small — in questions
of supreme importance and in the most apparently
insignificant decisions of daily life — live as one

who exists only so that the will of God and of Christ
may be carried out in him. It was to do God's will
that Christ came from heaven. It is to do God's will
in you that Christ has entered your heart. Beware
of hindering or grieving him in this, his blessed
work.

People sometimes ask, 'Didn't God give us a will
so that we could use it? Isn't having a will what gives
man his nobility? How can you ask us to give up
that will so entirely and absolutely to God?' What a
misunderstanding such questions reveal! God gave
us a will so that with it we might intelligently will
what he wills. A child is not degraded by giving up
his or her will in order to be guided by that of a wise
and loving father. So it is man's highest dignity to
find out and accept and delight in the perfect will of
God. We should consider it our true and only blessedness to let Christ breathe God's will into us. We
should never seek our own will in anything, and we
should instead let his will rule.

We need to accept Christ with a whole heart,
with a perfect will. You can have just as much of
Christ as you give of yourself to him: if you give
your whole heart, you can have the whole Christ.

The precondition of blessing in the Church is a
great breaking down in which Christians are made
to perceive how much they lack in their lives. At
some Bible conventions the speakers have become
so convicted of the evil and shame of their lives that
they have dared not speak in public without first
going to God and making confession. This sort of
conviction is what we need, what we cannot give
ourselves, and what God can work in us. It is a matter of shame and humiliation when a spouse is

unfaithful to the partner to whom he or she has pledged his or her whole heart. Similarly, the thought that we have been guilty of withholding from God the undivided love to which, as our Creator and Redeemer, he has such a perfect right, will make us bow down in the very dust. The sense of not having given our whole hearts to Christ will become unbearable. We need to confess that we have not given God his glory, that we have sought our own will and honour and pleasure, that we have given self and the world a place in the heart in which Christ wanted to dwell alone. Once God's Holy Spirit has shown us the sinfulness of our Christian lives, we will have no rest until we have said with real sincerity, 'I accept the whole Christ with my whole heart.' Then we will have the assurance of divine approval.

Believe that the indwelling Christ will do all that needs to be done in your heart

When Christ comes into our lives to take possession of us, by his Spirit he will do within us what we cannot do ourselves. He makes us what God wants us to be: conformed to the image of his Son. It is utterly vain for us to think of following Christ's steps or imitating his example or copying his life by any effort of our own. Jesus lived a human life upon earth so that he might show us how to live. But it is folly for us to think that simply because we are Christians we shall be able to achieve anything like his life. It is impossible. We are indeed called to imitate his life; it is our first duty. But we can fulfil that calling only if we let Jesus himself live his life in us. His life is altogether too high and too divine for us to reproduce. It is his own life, and his alone. But he will live it out in us.

You may want to be humble, or patient or gentle. How often you have prayed and struggled over this, but all in vain. You tried to achieve a perfection here on earth, in yourself, resembling that which Christ, as God, brought from heaven. What folly! Learn to turn away from self and its efforts. Turn inwards; let your faith be occupied with and rest in the Almighty Indwelling One, whose will is to fill you with his own life. Depend upon the One who dwells within you to do the work which he has undertaken.

He began his life upon the earth as a little baby, unknown and very feeble. He grew up in seclusion, and no one suspected that he was in fact the Redeemer of men. When he began his public ministry he did not lift up his voice in the streets; he was despised and rejected by men; they did not know that he was the Lord of Glory. Similarly, within your heart his appearance will to begin with be low and feeble and scarcely observable. This is the time when you must obey his command simply to believe. Trust in him with an unmeasured confidence; trust that he will do his work within you in his own way and time. However slow and hidden things seem to be within you, hold fast to your confidence that he is there, and that he is working, and that in due time he will reveal himself.

Dear Christians, when you believe in the incarnate Christ or the crucified Christ, it means that you believe that he perfectly accomplished the work which he came to earth to do, living and dying for you. When you believe in the risen and glorified Lord, it means that you have no shadow of doubt that he is now living and reigning at God's right hand in divine power. Let your faith in the indwelling Christ be just as simple and clear. He will carry out in wonderful power and love the work for which he entered your heart — the great work of possessing and renewing and glorifying your whole inner life. Trust him for this. The Christ of Bethlehem, the Christ of Calvary, the Christ of the Throne in Heaven, is the Christ who is in you. Begin to believe this: Jesus Christ is in me; Jesus Christ will do the work perfectly in me. Just listen to that wonderful promise in Hebrews: 'The God of peace ... make you perfect in every good work to do his will, *working in you* that which is wellpleasing in his sight, through Jesus Christ' (Heb. 13:20–21). *Yes, through Jesus Christ!* If it is through Christ that God works in you, how could he do this without Christ himself being in you? God enables you to do his will through the indwelling Christ. Doubt no longer, but rejoice. Know for yourselves that Jesus Christ is in you.

You may be asking, 'Can this really be? Oh, I wish I knew how I could have Christ himself dwelling in me.' What you need to do is simply this: give your heart to God. Have you truly done that? I do not ask whether you are a believer, whether you are sure that your sins are pardoned, whether you are seeking to live a Christian life. But have you given your heart to Christ so that he may possess it, rule it, renew it, fill it with the will of God and alone dwell in it? Have you given your heart away, out of your power and into his? Your self-confidence, your self-contentment, your self-pleasing, your self-will — has it all been laid at Christ's feet, so that he can cast it all out of you and fill you with himself? If not, let nothing keep you back from now giving to God what belongs to him, and what Christ came to win back for him.

Your heart was made for God. A human being has a wonderful ability to settle his heart in one moment upon some object which strongly attracts him or which has won his affection — he has an ability to give away his heart. Right now bow in penitence and shame, aware that you have little appreciated that Jesus Christ is in you and sorry that you have not truly yielded your whole being to him day by day. Bow in lowly confession, and offer him your sin-stained and unworthy heart, and believe that he will take possession of it. What you give, God takes; what God takes he will hold and keep through Jesus Christ. Blessed Lord, right now we give ourselves, and we know that you accept us, that you are within us, and that you will fill us with yourself.

Christ, Our Life

Christ, who is our life.
Colossians 3:4

This is a truth of infinite depth and richness. It lies at the very root of the Christian life, and leads into all its fullness and blessing. To understand it we must study it in three stages: Christ's life in the flesh on earth; Christ's life by the Spirit in the heart; and Christ's life in heaven working through us for the world.

The Christ-life in the flesh on earth

Before we can fully accept the Christ-life we must know what to expect from it — what it offers us, what its spirit and character is. We can only discover this from the life of Christ on earth. He lived in the flesh in order to make visible to us what the divine life is, to show us how a man ought to live with his God, how we will live when we have Christ as our life in us. It will help us if we study the divine life of Christ in the light of its root virtue — that is, *humility*.

He is the Lamb of God, meek and gentle and patient. It was a divine humility in heaven which moved him to come into the world as a servant: 'Being in the form of God ... [he] emptied himself, taking the form of a servant' (Phil. 2.6–7, RV). In true human humility he gave himself up to death on the cross: 'Being found in fashion as a man, he humbled himself, becoming obedient even unto death' (8). He said of himself, 'Learn of me; for I am meek and lowly in heart' (Matt. 11:29, RV). In him was fulfilled Zechariah's prophecy: 'Behold, thy king cometh unto thee ... lowly, and riding upon an ass' (9:9, RV). In everything he said about his Father he always spoke of his own entire dependence upon him. He could do nothing by himself (John 5:19, 30; 6:38; 7:16, 28, 40, 42; 8:28, 54; 12:49; 14:10, 24).

In all his dealings with men, in his bearing of reproach, injustice and suffering, in his readiness to help and serve, in his self-abasement and compassion, he always thought of himself as of no account. He did everything with the meekness, sweetness and gentleness of the Lamb of God. Humility is the root of his perfect character and atonement, and of the perfect life which he gives us.

Why does this have to be so? Because pride was

the one root of all sin, the cause of man's fall and of all disobedience. Pride had been the fall of the devil. In Paradise he breathed his poison into our first parents. Pride of knowledge, pride of will, pride of power, pride of life — it became the source of all rebellion against God, all selfishness and hatred amongst men, all darkness and discontent in the heart. Christ came to restore to us our right relation to God and to man. The only way he could do this was by his humility atoning for our pride, by giving us his humility instead of our pride, so that we might once again take our right place before God.

We can see this pride very clearly in his disciples — it was the root of their unbelief (John 5:44). How frequently Christ found it necessary to speak to them about humility (Matt. 18:1–4; 20:27; 23:11–12; Luke 14:11; 17:10; 18:14; 22:24, 26; John 13:16). Without this humility in Christ and in us, there is no salvation.

All Christians should look at their lives and compare them with Christ's humility. Let each one of us examine himself, and see how much of that humility he has attained. Before we can receive and desire and display the Christ-life we must appreciate our need of it. A deep humbling of our pride is the essential first step towards receiving the humility of Christ as a permanent trait of our lives (Rom. 12:3; 1 Cor. 13:4; Gal. 5:26; Eph. 4:2; Phil. 2:3; Col. 3:12; Jas. 4:6; 1 Pet. 5:6).

The Christ-life by the Spirit in our hearts

Once we know and hate and confess our own life

and its pride, it must then be crucified and killed.
The new life of humility must expel the old. Christ
the Stronger must cast out Pride the Strong. May
God reveal to us how much self has been in our
religion, and how nothing but the death to self in
the death of Christ can deliver us (Rom. 6:1–11;
Gal. 2:20; 6:14; Col. 2:20; 3:3). It is God's own
work to do this; our place is to wait before him in
helplessness and humility.

Then comes the claiming by faith of what Christ
is, the claiming of his life as ours. God's way is
always from the Outward to the Inward. All we
have seen of Jesus as One who is outside of us, we
may ask to be made ours within us — not as something which he gives us out of himself, but as something which he himself will be in us. Jesus is the Second Adam. Just as deeply, inwardly and essentially
as Adam and his sin has corrupted our nature and
dwelt and worked in us, Jesus the Second Adam
and his life can become ours. By faith we can have
the Son of God in his meekness dwelling in our
hearts (Gal. 2:20; 4:19; Eph. 1:20; 3:17).

Once we have by faith claimed this Christ-life as
our own, we wait on the Holy Spirit for the daily
revelation and renewal of what there is in the life of
Christ for us. As one need after another is dis-
covered, one grace after another is imparted.

In the case of the disciples, we see that even three
years of training and instruction in Christ's School
did little to teach them humility. Even at the Last
Supper there was an argument about who was the
greatest among them. The day of Pentecost
changed all that. The Holy Spirit brought down the
Heavenly Life in power, brought down the

glorified Jesus into their hearts, and their selfishness was changed into love.

Let us yield ourselves to the death of self, let us by faith claim Christ as our life, and live that life out in the power of the Holy Spirit. At the footstool of the throne of the exalted Jesus, the Holy Spirit comes to his waiting people (Acts 1:1–14; 2:1–4; 1 Cor. 6:19–20; Gal. 4:6; Rom. 8:2; 10:9).

The Christ-life in heaven working through us for the world

The Christ-life on earth had just one object: to glorify the Father by the salvation of the world. In heaven he works out that plan through everyone into whom his life enters. Look at the world now in the light of Christ's claims, promises, power and love. The power of the life of Christ is working in our churches and missions, in Christian school and social work, in the great Christian societies and in personal evangelism.

You have claimed the Christ-life and you are rejoicing in it or longing for it. Learn to see yourself as a consecrated bearer of the life that is the life of the world. Humility is the end of self — it is the willingness to seek nothing for yourself, to let God use you as he will. Look at the needs of the world, of the people you know, and commit yourself to a life of service. You have asked for the Spirit of the meek and gentle Lamb of God — be like him, a sacrifice.

God will teach each one of us how to let the Christ-life sustain and use us. May our hearts cry with intense desire, 'What is there, Lord, that I can

do, so that you may be better known and loved?'
And may we have faith that the Lamb of God will
dwell in our hearts, breathing his own Spirit into us.

6

Pleasing God

*… Having foreordained us unto adoption
as sons* through Jesus Christ *unto
himself, according to* the good pleasure
*of his will … having made known unto us
the mystery of his will, according to* his
good pleasure *which he purposed in him
… to sum up all things* in Christ.
Ephesians 1:5, 9–10, RV

The character and value of what a man does
depends upon what he is. The things we do can only
be well-pleasing to God if they are the expression of
a life and nature which is well-pleasing to him. And
because as God, he alone is the fountain and
possessor of all goodness, there is no possibility of

anything being well-pleasing to him unless he sees in it something of his own nature, accepted and brought to him by the creature.

In Christ, God has revealed what his will is and what his nature is. All his fullness and all his divine glory has been embodied and made manifest in Christ. And God can now have no fellowship with or delight in any thing or any creature unless he sees in it the likeness and the Spirit and the work of his beloved Son. All his good pleasure is in Christ Jesus. There is no way of being or doing what is well-pleasing to him except by bringing and offering to him something of his Son. To enter deeply into this is the secret of living a life which is well-pleasing to him.

This is clearly shown in our text. Our adoption as sons is *through Jesus Christ*, according to *the good pleasure* of God's will. The summing up of all things *in Christ*, with the sons of God as the first-born, is also according to *his good pleasure*. Our place in life as sons through Christ, our place and life in glory in Christ, is the good pleasure of God. So as we accept and act out this life, as we seek readiness for the glory in which all will be summed up in Christ, as we enter into this mystery of God's will and purpose and live in it, we shall become identified with what his good pleasure is, and we shall find that good pleasure resting upon us.

The practical application of this thought is very simple. God has only one will and purpose: that Christ should be all; that we should be sons through Christ; that all things (including ourselves) should be summed up in Christ as Head. God longs to see just one thing: that all should be in Christ. And we can do nothing more supremely well-pleasing to God than simply to yield ourselves utterly and entirely to Christ, to let him be all in us. We should not be afraid to say boldly to our Father, that just as he longs to see Christ in us, we yield ourselves to Christ, so that we may have as much of him in us as God is willing to give us. We should pray, 'Yes, my Father, let me — my heart, my life — be nothing but a vessel in which you may pour as much of Christ as you wish. You can have as much of me as you want, to fill me with the image and the Spirit of your beloved Son.'

If this surrender is made in simplicity and faith, the answer will not be held back. God will reply, 'My child, you have offered your whole self to me, to be filled with as much of Christ as is my will. I offer you my Son, so that you may be as wholly filled with him as you wish.' Yes, we may be sure that the Christian who looks up to God and is willing to die to self and its will, so that his heart may be filled with the Christ of God — the humble, self-denying, obedient Lamb of God — will know what it is to be pleasing to God. As he goes out of himself and lives in God's good pleasure, God's will, God's thoughts, God's promises and God's power, he will see by the Holy Spirit that there is no other condition as blessed as this, that this alone is the place where a child of God should dwell.

Dwelling here, he will find grace and strength to do the things which are pleasing to God, he will walk and work in the sunshine of his approval and love. He will understand that God himself is bringing about within him that which is pleasing in his sight, and that because of this his feeblest acts as a feeble child of God will truly be a source of infinite and unceasing pleasure to the Everlasting Father.

7

Love

The Lord make you to increase and abound in love one toward another, and toward all men, even as we do toward you ... ye yourselves are taught of God to love one another. And indeed ye do it toward all the brethren which are in all Macedonia: but we beseech you, brethren, that ye increase more and more.
1 Thessalonians 3:12, 4:9–10

Very often people go away from Christian meetings with a wonderful sense of the love which the believers have for one another. This love which they feel is really the very love of God, not natural human love. It is important that we understand and believe this, because the belief will lead us always to seek more of that love from God. If you had wings and could fly straight into the depths of the sun, you would find that the light which is always burning and shining there is exactly the same as the light which we have here upon earth. In the same way, the eternal, omnipotent love of God is the same love which binds Christians together into one, flowing through our hearts by the Holy Spirit. If we were indoors on a summer's day, we might say to ourselves, 'There is light here in this room, but outside, in the direct sunlight, it is brighter. I want to go outside and get all the sunshine I can.' Similarly, we want more of the divine love and want to stand in its full, direct light.

I want to draw your attention to the precious words of the Apostle Paul which are quoted above. He is writing to those who have only just been converted. He says they have been taught by God to love one another, and he says they have actually done it. Yet he tells them to increase in that love more and more. That should also be our aim today. We should pray that the Lord will make us 'increase and abound in love one toward another'.

Why is it that we Christians should be so happy when we meet together? We may come from different congregations and denominations, and yet we are happy when we are gathered together. This is because God has ordained that it shall be so. The fruit of the Holy Spirit is first of all love, and if our lives are full of the Spirit they will also be full of love.

How wonderful the holy, everlasting love of God is! His love never seeks its own good (1 Cor. 13:5), but always seeks the good of others. He loves to be the blessing of the creature. He delights in imparting his blessing, his purity and his glory to the whole universe. That is what our God is: a never-ceasing stream of everlasting love, flowing out to all. Out of his eternal goodness he created the universe. The sun, the moon, the stars, the trees, the flowers, the grass — they all demonstrate his power to make a beautiful world. After man had fallen, God said, 'I will send my Son, and I will let him die. I will give man my only beloved Son to dwell in his heart. Men shall share with me the happiness of having Christ as their own.'

The love of God

There is no source of light like the sun. It is always giving itself and sending out light. Scientists say that it is consuming itself and burning itself away in lighting the world. It is always sacrificing itself. This is also true of God in a far greater way. He too is always giving, is always the source of blessing to every being and every created thing. Our hearts can have no greater aim than just to be filled by this full, true, everlasting love of God, communicated to us by the Holy Spirit.

When I take a flame from a fireplace and put it among dry grass, the flame that was brought from the fireplace keeps its nature and sets fire to the grass. Similarly, the divine love comes into my heart and begins to burn – though sometimes feebly, since the tinder is often green. When we give ourselves up to God it is because his love has touched our hearts. The love which fills the Christian's heart is the very love of God, the fire of heaven burning within him.

When we meet fellow Christians we feel God's love flowing between us and them. But we should remember that we have as yet received only a small portion of God's love and light, and that we can receive the full light if we wish. That should be the object of our desire.

God's love is omnipotent. We know this through what it has done. A German hymn says, 'Love rent the heavens and came down to earth.' Love entered our humanity, and love carried Jesus through his wonderful thirty-three-year-long life on earth. Love went and gave itself up on the cross, shedding its blood and dying for us. Then love went to heaven to intercede for us, so that we might come near to God by the power of that love. Love enables Christ to do the work he has to do in the lives of millions of people upon earth. And this omnipotent love, when it enters your heart, does not change its nature. It is still omnipotent love, burning with divine fire.

It was the love of Christ which constrained the Apostle Paul to suffer and die for his fellow men. It was the love of Christ which, throughout the last eighteen centuries, constrained countless thousands of hearts to live and die for him. That love is the greatest power in heaven and earth. Let us take the beginnings of it which we already have in our hearts, and look for more of it by the power of God.

Oh, think of the power of love! Think what the heathen were in Rome eighteen centuries ago. Think what our forefathers in Europe were in pagan times. The love of Christ changed them.

Think of the heathen of recent times, and of how love has entered their hearts. Love has made cannibals, who had at one time drunk the blood of their enemies, accept Christ, and has then transformed them into his likeness.

Love is the power by which God changes your life. You may complain about your feebleness, your selfishness, your temper and so many other things, but there is a power which can change all that, if you are willing to let it. Let the Holy Spirit fill your heart, and your whole life will be transformed by the power which surpasses all knowledge. And even if you are happy in the love of Christ now, should it not be your life's endeavour to seek for more of that love? As Paul says, 'Ye yourselves are taught of God to love one another. And indeed ye do it ... but we beseech you, brethren, that ye increase more and more' (1 Thess. 4:9–10). So make it your life's endeavour to be filled with God's love.

A Christian lady was once working in Cape Town among the black people there. One tribe, the Fingoes, are looked upon as dogs by another tribe, the Kafirs, and there is an irreconcilable hostility between the two peoples. The lady brought a Fingo man to Christ, and told him that he must learn to love his enemies. She asked him if he thought he could love a man who had stolen his money. He hesitated for a moment, but then replied that he could love such a man. Then the lady, who was well aware of the hatred between the two tribes, said, 'Tell me, can you love a Kafir?' He replied at once, 'No, no! I cannot love a Kafir!' She began trying to persuade him, saying, 'But Christ Jesus died for you — his enemy!' But the man still replied, 'No, I cannot love a Kafir!' He and the lady parted then, but the truth she had spoken had entered into his heart. He came back the next week, and the conversation speedily returned to the old subject. 'Yes,' he said very solemnly, 'I see I must love a Kafir, but it is very hard.' 'Will you do it for Jesus?' asked the lady. 'Yes, I will do it for Jesus — I can love a Kafir now,' he replied. Jesus had changed his heart. The love of Christ works wonders, and it is the power which we need in order to please God in our daily lives.

Entering into the life of love

How can we enter into this life, in which we are empowered by the love of Christ? We can only enter into it if our hearts have first been filled with his love. I have often been told by people that despite praying persistently for that fullness of love, they have not received it. Often this is because they want to remain their own masters, and they want the Lord for their own comfort's sake — they only want him to give them peace and to take the sin and temper out of their hearts.

Let us take a painter as an example. If he wishes to paint a splendid picture, the canvas on which he puts the painting must be entirely his own. Will he be content to paint it on a piece of canvas belonging to someone else? No! And if his wife also wanted to use his canvas for some purpose or other he would say, 'No — I want the canvas to be wholly mine if I am to spend time and effort painting on it!' And that is what Jesus says to us. 'Do not ask me,' he says, 'merely to take away your temper or your lack of love, or whatever else it may be, so that you can still go around in the world as Christians who seek their own pleasure.' Just as the painter wants the canvas to be set apart for his work and the credit it will win him, so Christ wants us to give up our hearts and lives entirely to his service, glory and honour. If we are willing, he will say, 'Into this soul, entirely set apart for me, I will pour out the fullness of my love.' Jesus has come from heaven for nothing less than to bring the love of God into your heart and mine.

You have probably often read Ephesians chapter 3, where Paul says, 'I bow my knees unto the Father … that he would grant you, according to the riches of his glory, to be strengthened with might by his Spirit in the inner man; that Christ may dwell in your hearts by faith.' Hear what follows, and see what it means to receive the fullness of the love of Christ: 'that ye, being rooted and grounded in love, may be able to comprehend with all saints what is the breadth, and length, and depth, and height' of his love (verses 14, 16–18). It is his love which Christ brings into us. It was in the power of his love that his disciples became his witnesses in Jerusalem, in Samaria and unto the uttermost parts of the earth. He put his love in them in order that they might communicate it to others and that it might thus embrace the whole world.

If Jesus is willing to give us a love like that, we have to ask ourselves how we may obtain it. We must let the new nature take entire and complete possession of our souls. How is it that a great oak tree grows from a tiny acorn into its strength and beauty? Because it is in its nature to do so. For the same reason a lamb is gentle, a lion is fierce and a wolf is cruel. It is in the nature of man to be selfish and unloving. If I still have that nature within me, it is impossible for the divine love to enter my life. Receive the new nature by the power of the Holy Spirit. Let the love of God be born within you, let that love fill your whole being.

Let us give ourselves up to God, wholly and completely. Let us seek his wonderful, divine love. Dear brothers and sisters in Christ, we have this treasure within us. The vessels are made of mere earth — sometimes very fragile, very often broken — but there is nothing which delights God so much as pouring his treasure, his divine Son, into those vessels, the hearts and souls of men.

I have already likened God's love to the sun, and I will use the analogy again, since it is of immense value. The sun never wearies of shining, shining, shining. Whether we think of it or not, even if we hide ourselves from its searching light in a cave or close the doors and shutters of our houses, the sun still delights in shining on. And just so God delights in pouring down his omnipotent love upon our hearts every moment of every day, always longing to shine his light into us and through us. The feeble light of dawn turns our thoughts towards the sunshine of the daytime. Similarly, the fellowship with God which we have experienced so far in our lives points us towards the eternal love of God, which is longing to fill us. So let us open our hearts, let us give up everything to him. God wants to fill our hearts and lives with his love.

But you cannot obtain this new life without first

dying entirely to the old nature. Jesus himself could not get the resurrection life and the heavenly life of glory until he had laid down his earthly life, sinless and pure though it was. In just the same way, if you want the eternal love of God to take complete possession of your soul, the earthly life must be laid down at Christ's feet and brought to him as a sacrifice. Your will, your worldly wisdom, your temper — it must all be brought to him. Your own life, the self-life, must be surrendered to him entirely. His death must be accepted. His life and his love must be claimed. Then he will enter in and bring about the mighty change which is needed, and he will truly take possession of your heart. Believe in the omnipotence and nearness of the divine love. The next time you look at the sun, think of the power which God's love has to fill you with its light.

What a blessing and a privilege it is to witness and to work for Jesus in the power of his own love. Persevere in your work, and know that God's love and your heart fit together more exactly than any lock and key. Your heart was designed to contain the divine love. Just as a teacup is made to hold tea, a milk jug to hold milk and a kettle to hold water, so your heart was made to hold God's love. We often hear the words, 'the heart is the seat of the affections'; indeed, the heart is made to be a vessel and a temple of God's love. Let us make a covenant with God — a covenant of love. Let us tell him that we want our hearts to be filled with his love. Let us wait upon him quietly and prayerfully, and believe that he will do it.

8

Standing in the Gap

(Written in December 1914, during the Great War)

> *I exhort therefore, that, first of all,*
> *supplications, prayers, intercessions, and*
> *giving of thanks, be made for all men; for*
> *kings, and for all that are in authority;*
> *that we may lead a quiet and peaceable*
> *life in all godliness and honesty ... I will*
> *therefore that men pray everywhere,*
> *lifting up holy hands.*
>
> 1 Timothy 2:1, 2, 8

In the first chapter of this epistle Paul has spoken about himself and Timothy. In the remaining sections he goes on to deal with certain key questions about church leadership. In our text he mentions the call to prayer as something of pre-eminent importance. It is to him one of the chief marks of the Christian life, the true secret and test of its reality, the proof that it has power with God in heaven. He especially asks for prayer 'that we may lead a quiet and peaceable life in all godliness and honesty'. He believes that in circumstances of war or persecution prayer can succeed in bringing about peace, which is 'good and acceptable in the sight of God'. The old divines said, 'God rules the world by the prayers of his saints.' The words of Paul here give us the ground on which that statement rests. And they lead us to the question: Have we a right, in this present war, definitely to ask God to give peace in answer to the prayer of his people? Let us consider what Scripture teaches us.

When God made Adam in his image, it was so that he, like God, should be a king. He was to be God's viceroy, ruling and having dominion over the world which God had given him. After the Fall, God did not revoke his promise, but endeavoured to cultivate in the men whom he chose as his servants an awareness of *the voice they would have here on earth in the counsels of heaven.* It was God's aim to train them as kings and priests for the great work of intercession and blessing.

God resolved to tell his friend Abraham about the impending judgement of Sodom. Why? So that he might arouse within him a spirit of humble but bold intercession. God wanted to teach Abraham that he would listen to his intercession and would give an answer. It was Abraham's prayer which rescued Lot.

Time after time Moses had to pray that Pharaoh and Egypt might be freed from plagues. What was the meaning behind this? It was all intended to show that God's servant not only had the right to bring God's message to men, but also had the right to ask and to promise the mercy of the God whom he proclaimed. Similarly, on two occasions God threatened to cast off Israel. It was in response to Moses' determination to die rather than to see God reject his people that the Lord repented of what he had said and spared Israel. This taught Moses that of all the honours which had been bestowed upon him, this was the highest: *that God should listen to his voice and fulfil his desires*.

In the stories of the leaders, kings and prophets of Israel we have more than one instance of God giving deliverance and blessing upon hearing the voice of a man, even when he was ready to punish the people. But sadly, sometimes there was no voice to be heard. Think of what the Lord says in Ezekiel's prophecy: 'I sought for a man among them, that should make up the hedge, and stand in the gap before me for the land, that I should not destroy it: but I found none' (22:30; cf. Isa. 59:16, 62:6–7, 63:5, 64:7). The danger is that the land will be destroyed; the only hope is an intercessor; the terrible disappointment is that God cannot find one. And this is the final verdict: 'Therefore have I poured out mine indignation upon them' (Ezek. 22:31). This lesson reveals God's character and purpose to us, and gives us the assurance that when his servants on earth draw near to him in one accord with definite, believing requests, mercy will triumph over judgement.

So let us deal with the question of the present war as definitely and pointedly as we can. Can we ask God for a speedy peace? Surely Christ would answer, 'According to your faith be it unto you.'

What the Old Testament teaches us is all embodied in Christ Jesus. He had to identify himself with the race of Adam as the Son of Man, so that he might become the heir of the kingdom which Adam had lost. When he had accomplished his work, he rose to the throne of heaven, where he now lives for ever to intercede. He left his people, the members of his body, here on earth, *so that they might work with him in the task of intercession, and bring the needs of the world before God*. Let us believe that when we fully live in Christ, keeping his commandments and praying in his name, in answer to our prayers he will do greater things through us than he did when he was here upon earth. Mountains will be cast into the sea.

Let us all bring this petition to God: 'Lord, we beseech you, by your almighty power bring this war to an end, and graciously give us peace soon.' Let us remember that God is willing to do great things for the person who stands in the breach in the name of Christ. Let the prayer be prayed according to God's Word day and night, the unceasing habit of a soul which has devoted itself to pleading with God and giving him no rest, to stirring itself up and taking hold of him and saying (the words are provided for us in God's Holy Book), 'I will not let thee go, except thou bless me' (Gen. 32:26).

You may fear that this is too bold, beyond the reach of a child of Adam. But just think for a moment. God allows men like Napoleon, by virtue of that kingly power of ruling which he gave to Adam, but which has been so degraded by sin, to cause wars in which millions of lives are either sacrificed or plunged into the depths of suffering and sorrow. If he allows this, surely he will much rather allow the people of his Royal Priesthood to bring down peace and blessing on the suffering millions. Surely the prayer, 'In the midst of wrath, remember mercy' will touch his heart and in the name of Christ obtain the blessing.

Let us yield ourselves to the Holy Spirit for the task of intercession. It is not a simple, easy thing to offer our souls as a living sacrifice on behalf of our fellow men. But if we do it in the power of Christ, it will be a fruitful and blessed work.

As we look forward to our Christmas celebrations, let us take up the song of the angels, 'Glory to God in the highest!' And let us pray, 'On earth peace, and good will toward men' (Luke 2:14). Then, when we come to consecrate ourselves to God afresh at the New Year, let us vow that by his grace we shall yield ourselves more than ever before to testify to those around us about what our God is and what his claims are and how blessed it is to serve him. Let us vow to make his kingdom, by his almighty grace, the one object of our unceasing, fervent intercession, to bind heaven and earth into one at the foot of his throne.

O Holy Father, teach us to pray; teach us to believe; teach us to wait on you alone. O God of peace, for Christ's sake, give us peace in our time.

9

The Message of Romans

*I am not ashamed of the gospel of Christ:
for it is the power of God unto salvation
to every one that believeth; to the Jew
first, and also to the Greek.*

Romans 1:16

In the Epistle to the Romans Paul's exposition of
the gospel – which he calls 'the gospel of God' or
'the gospel of his Son' or 'my gospel' (1:1,9; 16:25)
– falls into four sections, to which we may assign the
following headings:

1. The Grace of Justification (1:18—5:11), or
Righteousness by Faith in Christ.
2. The Grace of Regeneration (5:12—8:39), or Life
in Union with Christ by Faith.

3. The Grace of Predestination (chapters 9—11),
or the Mystery of Faith.
4. The Grace of Sanctification (chapters 12—16),
or the Obedience of Faith.

If we consider these headings thoughtfully, we can
see that they depict the House of God as a great
cathedral in which the way of access to him is to be
found, in which he is to be worshipped, and from
which men are to go out and live their lives in this
world, wholly devoted to his service. The first of
the above sections reveals to us the foundation of
this great building. In the second section we have
the building itself rising up, 'an habitation of God
through the Spirit'. The third section may be com-
pared to a spire which points up towards heaven
and draws hearts and thoughts towards the One
whose ways are past finding out. And in the last section we have the walk of faith and obedience,
through which the believer grows, God is glorified
and the coming of his kingdom is brought nearer.

The Grace of Justification

Here we have the root and power of Paul's gospel.
He was especially raised up by God so that he might
bring this great message to the Jews, who had been
seeking salvation through the law, and to the Gentiles, who had been living without law. He first
depicts the state of the heathen world, and a very
dark picture it makes (1:18–32). The wrath of God
is being revealed from heaven against all the
ungodliness and unrighteousness of men. He then
proves that the Jews, with all their privileges and

their confidence in the law, are just as guilty before God as the heathens are (2:1—3:20). Having demonstrated that the whole human race is under sin, he closes with the terrible verdict that every mouth is silenced and the whole world is guilty before God (verse 19).

In all this Paul is digging deeply, so that the cathedral may be built strong and secure. In chapter 3 (verses 21–31) he reveals the four great cornerstones of the foundation: the righteousness of God, who justifies the sinner; the righteousness of Christ; the propitiation on which that righteousness rests; and the faith by which it is accepted.

In chapter 4 Abraham and David are appealed to as proof that in the Old Testament, faith was imputed as righteousness, and that the righteousness of faith was the only ground of acceptance by God. And then in the concluding portion of this section (5.1–11) Paul raises a shout of joy over the sure foundation which has been laid, as he speaks of the peace, grace, joy, hope and love secured for us in the death of Christ.

The Grace of Regeneration

In the first section Paul has shown that we are justified by Christ's death, and has remarked that 'much more, being reconciled, we shall be saved by his life' (5:10). So he now reveals what it means to be saved by Christ's life and explores the subject of life in Christ through faith. In this second section we find the words 'life' and 'live' eighteen times, and 'death' and 'dead' thirty-four times. Paul shows us that the new life of the believer is the superstructure which is to be built upon the foundation of justification.

Adam was our father — we had our life from him. In Christ, his antitype, we have new life. Our generation is from Adam; our regeneration is from Christ. All those who are justified by Christ not only live, but also reign in life through him (verse 17). Sin reigned in man's old, dead state; God's grace in Christ now reigns in the new, eternal life.

In chapter 6 Paul goes on to speak about our being united with Christ in his death and resurrection, so that we may have newness of life. Even as Christ lives a resurrection life, so are we to reckon ourselves dead to sin and alive to God in Christ Jesus. He ends the chapter with the words, 'The gift of God is eternal life.' In chapter 7 he then speaks of our being dead to the law so that we might be joined to Christ, in whom the law of the Spirit of life has made us free from the law of sin and death. Those who are in Christ can reign in life and triumph. This is the life, built upon the foundation of God's righteousness, in which the believer moves and works, bears and suffers, through the power of the Spirit of life in Christ Jesus.

The Grace of Predestination

In our text we have the words, 'to the Jew first, and also to the Greek'. Paul is now to speak about this great mystery of God's wisdom — namely, that he put the Jews first, and then, when they had refused his grace, cast them aside and turned to the Gentiles. I have said that this section is like the spire of the cathedral, pointing heavenwards. The spire reminds us that the House of God is above all a house for worship — a house for the deep, reverent adoration of God, even when we cannot understand his ways.

Paul points out how in the family of Abraham, in the cases of Isaac and Ishmael and of Jacob and Esau, the principle of election by God's grace was established. God is the potter, with sovereign power, to whom none may say, 'What do you think you are doing?' However, Israel, God's elect, had been disobedient, and deserved to be rejected. The Scripture had prophesied this, and the mystery behind it is now revealed: 'a hardening in part hath befallen Israel, until the fullness of the Gentiles be come in; and so all Israel shall be saved' (11:25–26, RV).

The apostle closes his plea for God with the words, 'O the depth of the riches both of the wisdom and the knowledge of God! How unsearchable are his judgements, and his ways past tracing out!' (11:33, RV). And he bows prostrate before this holy God: 'For of him, and through him, and unto him, are all things. To him be the glory for ever. Amen.' (verse 36 RV).

The Grace of Sanctification

This last section deals with the earthly walk and work of those who live in the Father's house. The opening verse sums up the character of this life in the world: 'Present your bodies a living sacrifice, holy, acceptable to God' (12:1). In chapter 6 we were taught how the fruit of righteousness in those who are made free from sin is sanctification — they are now holy to the Lord, possessed by the One who makes holy. In the second verse of chapter 12 Paul says that holiness is to do God's perfect will in everything, in the 'obedience of faith' (1:5, 16:26). In the rest of the chapter the various elements of the holy life — such as humility (verse 3) and love (9, 10) — are spelled out. In chapter 13 the law of love is again emphasised, beginning with subjection to the higher powers. The true life is defined as a putting aside of the flesh and a putting on of Jesus Christ. In chapter 14 the law of love in relation to our brethren who differ from us is expounded, and in chapter 15 (verses 1–7) this is summed up in the command to please our neighbour rather than ourselves, 'for even Christ pleased not himself' (verse 3).

The Roman Christians are then encouraged to think of the larger world in which Paul has been labouring (verses 8–21) and are urgently called to join him in his struggle by praying for him. In the last chapter the message of love is underlined by the apostle's example in his greetings to all who know him at Rome. And the epistle concludes by giving praise to God: 'Now to him that is able to stablish you according to my gospel ... to the only wise God, through Jesus Christ ... be the glory for ever. Amen.'

10

Through Christ Jesus

> *We ... rejoice in God through our Lord*
> *Jesus Christ, through whom we have*
> *received the reconciliation.*
>   Romans 5:11, RV

If after studying the character of Paul one were asked to say what its chief trait was, one would find it difficult to give any answer other than this: the intense reality of the presence of Jesus Christ. Just notice how often he mentions the name of Christ, even where it does not appear to be strictly necessary to do so. See how he relates all that he has to say about God, the spiritual life and his own life and work to his blessed Lord. One can clearly see that Christ possessed his heart and thought and filled his whole being. Whether we look at his teaching, his practical instructions to believers or his personal testimony, everything centres on Christ. 'Christ is our life,' says Paul; 'to me to live is Christ'; 'Christ liveth in me'.

Let us take the Epistle to the Romans as an example. After he has expounded the great truth of justification by faith (3.21—4.25), Paul speaks about the blessedness of the man who is justified: 'Therefore being justified by faith, we have peace with God *through our Lord Jesus Christ*' (5:1). Then there follow the words, 'By whom also we have access by faith into this grace wherein we stand, and rejoice in hope of the glory of God.' The peace and the grace and the joy are all linked to Christ. Then, after we have read that 'while we were yet sinners, Christ died for us' (verse 8), we find that 'Much more then, being now justified by his blood, we shall be saved from wrath *through him* ... And not only so, but we also joy in God *through our Lord Jesus Christ*' (9, 11). It is not merely faith and justification which give us peace and joy; we have to remember constantly that it all comes through personal fellowship with the living Jesus Christ as he lives his life in us.

Notice how this centrality of Christ is taken up and expanded into a new meaning in the rest of Romans. In chapter 5 (verses 12–21) we read of the abundance of grace, which, once received, enables the believer to reign in life *through Jesus Christ*. The conclusion states that 'as sin reigned in death, even so ... grace [reigns] through righteousness unto eternal life *through Jesus Christ our Lord*' (21, RV). Then in chapter 6, after seeing the name of

Jesus and our union with him mentioned many times, we have the exhortation to reckon ourselves 'alive unto God *through Jesus Christ our Lord*' (1–11). And once again at the end of the chapter: 'The free gift of God is eternal life *in Christ Jesus our Lord*.'

Chapter 7 begins with our being dead to the law through the Body of Christ, so that we should be 'joined to another, even to him who was raised from the dead' (4, RV). Then Paul goes on to show how this separation from the law is realised in the believer who cries out, 'O wretched man that I am! Who shall deliver me from body of this death? I thank God *through Jesus Christ our Lord*' (7:24–25). Chapter 8 teaches us what that deliverance by Christ is, and shows us the marks of the law of the Spirit of life in Christ Jesus, which makes us free from the law of sin and death. This leads us on at the close of the chapter to a shout of victory: 'We are more than conquerors *through him that loved us*. Neither death nor life ... shall be able to separate us from the love of God, which is *in Christ Jesus our Lord*'.

As water is carried through a pipe, so all the fullness of salvation is received and enjoyed, from stage to stage, *through Jesus Christ our Lord*. This illustration will help us to take in one of the deepest secrets of Paul's teaching in Romans. Too often people are content with the earlier part of the epistle's wonderful revelation that we are justified freely by God's grace through the redemption which is in Christ Jesus and his propitiation of our sin (see especially 3.21–26). And so Christ's work for us on the cross, and God's work of justifying us for Christ's sake, are regarded as the all-sufficient strength of the Christian life. The believer does not come to a full understanding of the truth that the personal life and fellowship of Jesus Christ are his only hope and confidence. When the water is brought into a house, and each tap is expected to work properly, everything depends upon the pipe being built into the house and maintaining, in unbroken continuity, the connection with the reservoir. Similarly, it is through Jesus Christ that the Holy Spirit, the water of life, and the abundant grace of God can be received in every moment of the Christian's experience.

Let us look again at some of the verses from Romans which we have quoted and see how everything depends upon our personal relationship to Christ being maintained as continuously as is our contact with the air which we breathe. When we read that we are justified by faith and have peace with God, let us remember that the experience of that justification and peace can only be had *through our Lord Jesus Christ*. It is through him that 'we have access by faith into this grace wherein we stand and rejoice' (5:2). Likewise, in the fuller experience of the abundance of grace we 'reign in life *by one, Jesus Christ*' (5:17). Christians often struggle and pray to have their consciousness of their justification made clear and permanent, so that they may have peace and joy. And yet they do not understand that their prayer can only be answered, and all they desire can only be received, through Jesus Christ, the living Saviour. He will keep up that unceasing fellowship which he has promised and which the Holy Spirit will make real in the heart.

Let us try to take hold of this truth. Faith in what Christ has done on Calvary is the initial stage, and absolutely indispensable to peace with God and joy in him. But this is only the gateway. In our daily lives, as this faith in Christ grows stronger and deeper, we shall discover for ourselves the truth that not only was Christ made sin for us, but also we have been made the righteousness of God *in him*. Our faith, which was to begin with fixed upon his redemption and our justification, grows into its fullness as we see that Jesus Christ takes hold of us, keeps charge of us, keeps us from the power of sin and keeps the fullness of his life and Spirit and blessing flowing into us and through us. And so 'through Christ Jesus' becomes the watchword of our lives.

11

The Reign of Grace

> *Where sin abounded, grace did abound
> more exceedingly: that, as sin reigned in
> death, even so might grace reign through
> righteousness unto eternal life through
> Jesus Christ our Lord.*
>
> Romans 5:20–21, RV

In his life Paul was the perfect embodiment and living witness of what God, in his grace, could do for a sinner. Paul's teaching is full of the glory of the reign of the grace of God. In the Epistle to the Romans we can find a complete exposition of the place which grace takes in the gospel — 'the gospel of the grace of God', as Paul calls it.

In the opening verses of Romans we find this

salutation: 'Grace to you and peace from God our Father, and the Lord Jesus Christ' (1:7). Grace is the first word which we meet in the gospel of God. It bids us to look up and remember that God meets us and waits for us with just one purpose — to show in us the immeasurable riches of his grace. Grace bids us to surrender ourselves joyfully to the God who has undertaken to do for us, every moment of our lives, everything that we need in order to please him and to be happy ourselves. We can rest assured that God, in his love, has done and will do all that is needed to make us his children in Christ Jesus. In the Lord Jesus Christ the infinite God has revealed and brought near and imparted to us his full grace and truth, so that we might receive it all. Let these opening words of Romans be to us the opening of each reading from God's word, of every act of praise and prayer, of every new morning and every new deed. 'Grace to you and peace,' says Paul; let our faith say 'Amen'.

In chapter 3 Paul speaks about the first great gift of grace: the righteousness of God, revealed in Christ. We are 'justified freely by his grace through the redemption that is in Christ Jesus' (3:24). Salvation is all by grace, from the first step of full pardon and reconciliation with God to the last stage, in which we enter into the inheritance of the saints. And everything in between — our being sanctified and made ready to serve and glorify the Lord — is by grace too.

In chapter 5 we have a new thought: 'being justified by faith, we have peace with God through our Lord Jesus Christ: by whom also we have access by faith into this grace wherein we stand, and rejoice

in hope of the glory of God' (5:1–2). Through our
Lord Jesus Christ we not only have peace with
God, but we also have grace to live for him joyfully.
As a tree stands and lives by its roots in the soil, so
we are planted in grace, and can stand rejoicing in
the hope of glory — more than that, we can rejoice
in the midst of sufferings. We have been brought
into a life in which we may in every moment depend
upon the riches of God's grace to fill us with an
indescribable, glorious joy.

Grace not only saves us from the guilt of sin by
the righteousness which it bestows, but it also saves
us from the power of sin by the new life which it
gives us. We must always remember that grace is
more than God merely giving us unmerited favour.
It is also the divine energy or power which works in
us every moment of our lives. In the second half of
chapter 5 (verses 15–17) Paul contrasts this new life
to the old life which we have in Adam, which is
tainted by sin and death. He draws a parallel
between the trespass and the free gift, and shows us
that not only are we delivered from the trespass and
its consequences, but also the grace of God and
grace's gift of the 'one man, Jesus Christ' does
much more than this: 'If, by the trespass of the one,
death reigned through the one; much more shall
they that receive the abundance of grace and of the
gift of righteousness reign in life through the one,
even Jesus Christ' (5:17, RV). It is not only that
grace will prevail over sin and life over death, but
such will be the abundance of grace that those who
receive it will *reign in life* through Jesus Christ.
Grace is life; grace is life reigning in divine power,
even here upon earth. Grace not only brings us

peace and pardon and joy in the hope of glory, but it also makes us kings reigning in life over the power of sin through Jesus Christ.

At the end of this passage the glory of grace is revealed still more wonderfully: 'The law came in beside, that the trespass might abound; but where sin abounded, grace did abound *more exceedingly*' (5:20–21, RV). Not only on Calvary, not only throughout the world in a general sense, but in every heart, sin abounded. But where sin abounded, there grace abounded all the more, making the heart the scene of its mighty wonders and rendering it fit to be the very dwelling of God, 'that, as sin reigned in death, even so might grace reign through righteousness unto eternal life through Jesus Christ our Lord.' All that we can possibly know of the terrible reign of sin in the heart is nothing but a prophecy and a pledge of what grace can do within us. Paul's whole experience confirms this.

Let us make sure that we have taken in the full meaning of the verses in Romans which we have been considering. 'Grace to you and peace from God our Father, and the Lord Jesus Christ.' This shows us that the whisper of the Holy Spirit can fill our hearts with its blessing and enable us to live our lives under its power. 'Being justified freely by his grace'; this means that the Holy Spirit can teach us, in our every approach to God, amidst all our consciousness of our sin and unworthiness, to believe that the righteousness which grace has bestowed is always ours, giving us full access to God and acceptance in his sight. 'By whom ... we have access by faith into this grace'; this tells us that as we believe in Christ Jesus and cling to him, he gives us entrance, ever new and deeper, into the grace in which we rejoice, hoping for the glory of God. We learn that grace is really meant to be as natural to us and as inseparable from us as the air we breathe, as active and triumphant in our lives as sin has ever been. Oh, how wonderful it is to experience grace as our daily breath.

And when we learn to know this grace in its abundance we shall learn to believe that 'reigning in life' over sin is indeed our inheritance, and with our whole lives we will sing: 'As sin hath reigned unto death, grace reigns through Jesus Christ unto eternal life.'

What a need there is to exert ourselves in the faith which lives and moves and has its being in this divine, heavenly, supernatural grace, and rejoices in it as if it were a sun which never sets.

12

Sin and Grace

What shall we say then? Shall we
continue in sin, that grace may abound?
God forbid.

Romans 6:1

In the previous chapter of Romans (verse 20) Paul
has made the bold statement that the law was given in
order that sin might abound. The thought might now
arise that if it is true that the holy and spiritual law,
given by a holy and righteous God, was meant to make
sin abound, might it not be the case that grace may
have the same purpose, in order that it might all the
more prove how full and free and sovereign grace is?

Some think that the question asked by Paul is
intended to meet an objection made either by the

enemies of the gospel or by Christians who were seeking an excuse for sin. But might it not be that the question is suggested to him by the thought of what may be in the minds of his readers? Since he has so magnified the grace of God, which is so much more abundant than sin, the question naturally arises, How is it that this abundant grace does not now conquer the sin in us? If Paul is trying to face this question, his answer will address one of the greatest difficulties in the Christian life and will open up the real mystery of what grace can do.

Indeed, Paul wishes to show us that it is in the very nature of grace to conquer sin. He has said that grace reigns through Jesus Christ; he now points out that it is only in a real and living union with him that sin's power is broken, and he makes it clear that where sin is not overcome, this can only be because Jesus Christ, in the power of his death, is not fully known. Let us note the great steps of this argument.

In our baptism we were baptised into Christ's death to sin. The death of Christ was the most important thing in his life; everything culminated there. It is not enough for us to be baptised into him as the divine Babe in Bethlehem, or as the man who was himself baptised with water and with the Holy Spirit and with fire; it is not enough to be baptised into him as the Christ of God, mighty in word and deed, or into all the love and compassion which he gave to men throughout his whole life. It is only in his death to sin that our redemption is to be found. We were baptised into his death. By identifying with his death, we have become united with him and have passed through all that he did. This, and nothing less than this, is the grace which has triumphed over sin.

We can be one with Christ in the power of his resurrection life only by knowing that our old self has been crucified with him, so that our flesh might be made powerless and so that we might no longer be in bondage to sin. It is by the power of fellowship with Christ's death that the power of sin is actually and practically broken. The death which Christ died, he died to sin once; the life which he lives, he lives unto God. We are to reckon ourselves as he is — dead to sin but alive to God.

Here we have the deep, full and blessed answer to the question, Must we still continue in sin in order to prove how abounding grace is? God forbid — *we are dead to sin*. He who understands and believes this truth and wholly yields himself to it will begin to know the abounding riches of grace. He will find that where sin used to abound in his life, there day by day grace will abound even more than sin did.

Shall we, must we, need we continue in sin in order that grace may abound? This thought troubles many hearts, even in our times. And many more are not troubled by it simply because they have not given themselves up to the hopeless realisation of the impossibility of not sinning every day. The one great answer which Paul gives to the question is just the gospel which is needed in the Church of our day. To be dead to sin in Jesus Christ, to be crucified with him, to have the whole Spirit and disposition of Christ, as revealed on the cross, living and working in us — it is in this that the glory of God's grace is seen, it is in this alone that we will find that those who receive the abundance of grace reign in life through Christ Jesus.

Paul closes the first half of chapter 6 with the

words, 'Reckon ye ... yourselves to be dead indeed unto sin, but alive unto God through Jesus Christ our Lord' (verse 11), thus summing up his teaching that 'we have been planted together in the likeness of his death' (5). Since this is true, he commands his readers, 'Let not sin therefore reign' (12). It might be argued that these words would be better placed at the very beginning of the chapter, following the statement, 'As sin hath reigned unto death, even so might grace reign through righteousness unto eternal life by Jesus Christ our Lord' (5:21). But Paul's argument would then be incomplete, since at the start of chapter 6 he has not yet revealed the power which makes it possible for him to say, 'Let not sin reign' and for us to obey the command. Only once we have understood the teaching that we are baptised into Christ, dead to sin in him and planted with him in the likeness of his death — only when we have appreciated that our old self has been crucified with him, so that the body of sin no longer has any power — can we with confidence respond to the command, 'Let not sin reign'!

The great achievement of grace in triumphing over sin and enabling us to triumph is this: that through it Christ himself, the living Saviour in the power of his cross, becomes our life. It was in the power of the Holy Spirit that he offered himself as a sacrifice to God. By that very same Spirit we are baptised into his death, and he becomes the mighty power which separates us from sin and self. It is by that same Spirit that the living Christ is revealed within us each day and each hour as the power which has conquered sin and which keeps possession of the house from which the strong man has been cast out. It is this teaching that we need not sin because grace abounds which becomes the power of a fruitful life.

13

Paul's Prayers for a Convention

*For what thanksgiving can we render
again unto God for you, for all the joy
wherewith we joy for your sakes before
our God; night and day praying
exceedingly that we may see your face,
and may perfect that which is lacking in
your faith?*
1 Thessalonians 3:9–10, RV

In Paul's First Epistle to the Thessalonians we find what we might call his programme for a convention. In the verses quoted above we first of all have thanksgiving and joy filling Paul's heart as he remembers what God has done for the Thessalonians, and how he has looked after them and blessed them. Next we read that he is praying ceaselessly that he may be able to see them and minister to them. He longs to be with them, to have a convention or coming together with them. Then he goes on praying, 'Now may our God and Father himself, and our Lord Jesus, direct our way unto you. And the Lord make you to increase and abound in love one toward another, and toward all men, even as we also do toward you; to the end' — this is the object of the prayer — '[that] he may stablish your hearts unblameable in holiness before our God and Father, at the coming of our Lord Jesus with all his saints' (verses 11–13, RV).

Thanksgiving and joy

These verses suggest to us five key thoughts about the Christian conventions which we attend. The first thing is thanksgiving and joy. Paul is coming to them with a heart overflowing with happiness. He was afraid that the tempter might have tempted them, but he has had news from them that they are abounding in faith. So now he is rejoicing in God and asks, 'What can I give as a thanksgiving to God for all the joy he has given me?' And that is the right spirit for a convention. We should begin by praying to God that we, his children, his saints, his redeemed ones, may meet together to rejoice in his presence. May God give us that joy, and remove everything which might hinder it, so that it may become the key note of our lives.

Ceaseless prayer

Paul says that he is praying for them 'night and day exceedingly'. That is the second thing we need to think about. It means that Paul had such a vision of the blessing which fills heaven, such a vision of the heavenly power, greatness, holiness and strength which these people needed — that he could not help praying night and day, 'O God, bless them and bring me to them so that I may be a blessing to them.'

When I was at Keswick in England, the thing which struck me most of all was the atmosphere of prayer which existed there. Earnest Christians had for a long time before been praying continuously and fervently, and they came to the convention with great expectations. They had asked God for a great deal and were confident that there would be a blessing, and even people who had not been praying came under the influence of it. We should take this as an example for the all conventions which we attend in the future. Let us take Paul's words as our rule, and let us pray 'night and day exceedingly' for those conventions. You can pray all through the day; you can even do it when you wake up in the night — 'God, please give your blessing to the convention; bless my soul, fill me with your Spirit and your joy; bless every meeting.' And while you are at the convention, you can pray all the time, as you go into the meetings, during the meetings and as you go out from them. Oh, it is a wonderful thing that God can be so near to his children! Once a Christian understands that truth, amidst all his work and care and joy he can be praying all the time, 'You are so near to me; I am looking for you.'

The perfecting of faith

Paul tells the Thessalonians, 'we ... [are] praying exceedingly that we may see your face, and may perfect that which is lacking in your faith'. He felt that their faith needed teaching, quickening and enlarging. He believed that it was incomplete, but he trusted that by the grace of God he would be able to perfect it. Faith, then, is the third subject we want to consider.

Why do we come to conventions? In order to get our faith strengthened and perfected! What is the great hindrance to this? If we were to ask the Lord Jesus, he would answer, 'your unbelief'. God's promises are so full, and he will fulfil them to us; God's provision for our lives is so wonderful, and he will bestow that provision — but our unbelief so often separates us from it. God said to Abraham, 'I am God Almighty — trust me.' And Abraham did — 'He was strong in faith, giving glory to God.' Do you go to conventions with that attitude, expecting God to fulfil his promises in your life and in the lives of others? Or do you come lacking faith and joy? May God help us to understand that at a convention the first and last thing is faith in God.

The story of the Keswick Convention in England is worth telling. Its founder, Canon Battersby, once heard a sermon on the power that a Christian can have simply by trusting in Christ's power and word. The sermon was based on this verse in John's Gospel: 'Go thy way; thy son liveth. And the man believed the word that Jesus had spoken unto him'

(4:50). The man had nothing but the word of Christ, but he went back to Capernaum happy, confident that what Christ had promised had happened, that his son had been restored. After hearing that sermon Canon Battersby struggled with God until he saw it all. 'I just have to believe in the power of Jesus, and I will get the victory,' he thought. From that night on his life was transformed, because he had come to understand what faith was. A year later he invited some people to come to the very first Keswick Convention, and there he simply told them what God had done in his life. Then he and some others endeavoured to pass on that blessing, and since then Keswick has passed it on to countless thousands in England.

Just to receive and believe the word of Christ — that is what we need to do. What a change there is in the life of the believer if he gets a word from the Lord through a speaker at a convention and he begins to see that all he has to do is trust God! That is a worthy aim for a convention — that if the people lack faith, they may be perfected in faith. Let it be our prayer at the conventions which we attend that God will give the preachers grace to speak so clearly and so personally to the need of the soul, that our faith may be strengthened and our hearts stirred to take God at his word and expect him to fulfil it.

Abounding in love

Paul prays, 'And the Lord make you increase and abound in love one toward another, and toward all men, even as we also do toward you.' This is our fourth thought. Note the order here. The first was joy and thanksgiving; the next was unceasing prayer; the next was faith; and now comes love. In chapter 4 Paul says, 'Concerning love of the brethren ye have no need that one write unto you: for ye yourselves are taught of God to love one another; for indeed ye do it toward all the brethren which are in all Macedonia. But we exhort you, brethren, that ye abound more and more' (verses 9–10, RV). He has heard that they are full of love, but he urges them to increase in that love.

Love — it is the great secret of the Christian life. God is love; Christ is love; the Holy Spirit sheds abroad the love of God. The true, happy, holy, humble Christian life is a life of love. We are not merely talking about a love towards God, or a faith in God's love towards us, but also a love for each other, a love for the hungry, a love for those who are in Christ which does not judge or despise.

It is an easy thing to say, 'Lord, make me increase and abound in love,' but it is not so easy to face up to the question, 'Why is it that I cannot get rid of all that unloveliness, that temper and sharp judgement, that contempt for some people?' God uses that deep sense of lack of love to bring about a change in us. At the Keswick Conventions thousands of people have been blessed by a conviction which makes them say in their hearts, 'My Christian life may be very impressive and earnest and devoted to God's work, but I know I don't have God's love inside me. There is so much impatience, selfishness, bad feeling and wrong thinking!' Many people who go to Keswick to find comfort and happiness actually become more wretched and miserable than ever before there, and they are made so aware of how little love there is in their hearts that they begin to despair of themselves. However, this very despair then reveals itself to be the path to new life.

Let us pray that at the conventions we attend in the future the Lord will make us all full of love, and let us ask him to show us if there is anything in our hearts which does not love and cannot love. Let us ask him to break it away from us, and let us wait patiently until he himself gives us his heart of love. God can do it! Pray to him for it. May the Lord make us abound and increase in love. Ask it of the Almighty God for yourself.

Established in holiness

Then the fifth and last thing we want to think about is holiness. Paul prays that God will establish the Thessalonians' hearts 'unblameable in holiness'. What a prayer! Isn't that just what you long for? Just imagine what it would be like to have a heart established by God's power, rooted and unblameable in holiness! But surely Paul cannot have meant it, we think. We are always ready to say, 'It cannot be.' But he did mean it — he would not have prayed for it if he had not believed that God could and would do it. In chapter 5 he prays, 'And the God of peace himself sanctify you wholly; and may your spirit and soul and body be preserved entire, without blame' (verse 23, RV). Then he adds, 'Faithful is he that calleth you, who will also do it.'

So if you want to pray for a Christian convention, here is the list of prayer priorities which is suggested by Paul: pray night and day that among the Christians there might be joy and thanksgiving to God, that faith may have right of way among them and may be made perfect in them, that their love may increase and abound, and that unblameable holiness may become their possession as God's children.

The African Evangelical Fellowship

The African Evangelical Fellowship is an international evangelical mission. This book is published in association with them. It had its beginnings in the challenge of missionary outreach in South Africa in the 1880s. Together with Spencer Walton, Andrew Murray was God's man to accept this challenge and the work of the South African General Mission began in Capetown in 1889. Andrew Murray was the president of the S.A.G.B. until his death in 1917. Since then, over 1300 missionaries have served in 13 different countries of Southern Africa under the S.A.G. and A.E.F., as the mission has been known since 1961. Today over 360 missionaries are still active in Africa serving with those churches established under past ministries. For more information about their work, please contact them at their International Office, 35 Kingfisher Court, Hambridge Road, Newbury, Berkshire RG14 5SJ, England.

Other AEF offices are:-

Australia
PO Box 292
Castle Hill
New South Wales 2154

Zimbabwe
99 Gaydon Road
Graystone Park
Borrowdale
Harare

Canada
470 McNicoll Avenue
Willowdale
Ontario M2H 2E1

South Africa
Rowland House
6 Montrose Avenue
Claremont 7700

USA
PO Box 2896
Boone
North Carolina 28607

New Zealand
PO Box 1390
Invercargill

United Kingdom
30 Lingfield Road
Wimbledon
London SW19 4PU

Europe
5 Rue de Meautry
94500 Champigny-sur-Marne
France